Science at the Edge

Cloning

Sally Morgan

Heinemann
LIBRARY

www.heinemann.co.uk/library
Visit our website to find out more information about **Heinemann Library** books.

To order:
☎ Phone 44 (0) 1865 888066
📄 Send a fax to 44 (0) 1865 314091
🖥 Visit the Heinemann Bookshop at www.heinemann.co.uk/library to browse our catalogue and order online.

First published in Great Britain by Heinemann Library, Halley Court, Jordan Hill, Oxford OX2 8EJ, a division of Reed Educational and Professional Publishing Ltd. Heinemann is a registered trademark of Reed Educational and Professional Publishing Ltd.

OXFORD MELBOURNE AUCKLAND JOHANNESBURG BLANTYRE
GABORONE IBADAN PORTSMOUTH NH (USA) CHICAGO

© Reed Educational and Professional Publishing Ltd 2002
The moral right of the proprietor has been asserted.

Designed by Tinstar Design (www.tinstar.co.uk)
Illustrations by Art Construction
Originated by Ambassador Litho Ltd.
Printed and bound in Hong Kong/China

ISBN 0 431 14882 1
06 05 04 03 02
10 9 8 7 6 5 4 3 2 1

British Library Cataloguing in Publication Data
Morgan, Sally
    Cloning. – (Science at the edge)
    1.Cloning – Juvenile literature
    2.Cloning – Moral and ethical aspects – Juvenile literature
    I.Title
    660.6'5

Acknowledgements
The Publisher would like to thank the following for permission to reproduce photographs:
Holt: p34; Imagestate: p40; Kobal: p8; Liz Eddison: p13; NHPA: p12; Oxford Scientific Films: pp48, 50, 54; Popperfoto: p21; Science Photo Library: pp4, 7, 9, 10, 15, 17, 20, 28, 30, 32, 33, 36, 39, 42, 45, 52, 57; Telegraph Colour Library: p27.

Cover photograph reproduced with permission of Science Photo Library.

Our thanks to Dr Michael Winson for his assistance in the preparation of this book.

Every effort has been made to contact copyright holders of any material reproduced in this book. Any omissions will be rectified in subsequent printings if notice is given to the Publisher.

Any words appearing in the text in bold, **like this**, are explained in the Glossary.

11.99 D

**Books are to be returned on or before
the last date below.**

17. NOV 2004

19. MAY 2005

29. OCT 2007

LIBREX —

Contents

Introduction

On 5 July 1996, Dolly the sheep was born. Dolly became the most famous sheep in the world. The reason for her fame was that she was a clone – she was genetically identical to her mother, a sheep that was born six years earlier. This means that Dolly was born with exactly the same **genes** as her mother. This was a major achievment in the field of **genetics**, the biological equivalent to splitting the atom or breaking the sound barrier. Before Dolly's birth, many scientists thought it was impossible to clone an adult cell. Since her birth, the potential development of cloning technology has both excited and worried people – scientists and non-scientists alike.

Dolly is probably the best known sheep in the world. She was the first clone of an adult cell to be produced. She is a perfectly normal sheep and has led a relatively healthy life, although she has begun to suffer from arthritis.

What is cloning?

Cloning is the creating of a genetically identical copy of an individual. Cloning itself is not new. Identical human twins are natural clones. Just after **fertilization**, the newly formed cell splits into two identical halves and each half continues to develop normally. The result is two identical people or clones. Normally, children of the same parents have different appearances. They are similar in that half their genes come from their father and the other half from their mother, but the actual mix of genes in each case is different. Identical twins also have genes from each parent, but in their case the genes are the same. Gardeners have been producing clones of plants, too. They produce new plants by taking cuttings. The cuttings develop into plants that are identical to the parent plants. They call this vegetative propagation, but it is the same as cloning.

Cloning concerns

Cloning raises a wide range of issues. Scientists and many other people believe that, if carefully regulated, the scientific technique of cloning could be used to benefit people. For example, cloning offers hope to many people suffering from diseases such as **Parkinson's** and **leukaemia**. Many people who contract leukaemia need a **bone marrow transplant**. They may be lucky and have a close relative that has compatible cells. Otherwise they have to hope somebody on a bone marrow register (a list of potential **donors**) has suitable cells. But the chances of finding a match are fewer than one in 20,000. Cloning could change that. Doctors could use a cloning technique to produce bone marrow cells that would be identical to the patient's own.

However, the issue of human cloning is one that concerns many people, both scientists and non-scientists. Some fear the consequences if doctors or scientists are able to produce human clones, including the possibility of health defects, and there are many **ethical** and religious objections which you will read about.

In this book you will learn about **DNA** and **chromosomes** and the difference between cloning in plants and animals. You will discover how cloning may be used in transplant surgery, and read about some of the issues associated with the cloning of human cells. You will also find the answers to questions such as 'Is Dolly the only cloned animal?', 'Is it legal to clone humans?' and 'Could the dead be cloned?'

The path to Dolly

Dolly the sheep was born in July 1996. The research institute where she was born kept the news of her birth secret until February 1997. When the news was finally released, it made headlines around the world. In the months that followed, cloning was rarely out of the news. Although there was a great deal of excitement, the news also raised concerns about the potential implications of this major advance in our knowledge of **genetics**.

People have thought about cloning for thousands of years, long before there was knowledge of genetics or biochemistry. However, it wasn't until towards the end of the 19th century, when scientists began to study **embryology** using microscopes, that the relevant science began to develop. One of the most important embryologists of this time was Hans Spemann, a Nobel Prize winner, who published his book *Embryonic Development and Induction* in 1938. He took from a salamander (a type of amphibian), an **embryo** that consisted of just two cells and split it into two. Each of the embryos developed into a normal salamander. They were identical copies or clones of each other. In his book, he proposed doing a fantastical experiment which would involve removing a **nucleus** from an adult salamander cell and placing it in an egg which had had its nucleus removed. But it was not until 1952, years after his death, that this experiment was carried out successfully.

Eggs, tadpoles and toads

During the 1950s, scientists Robert Briggs, Tom King and later John Gurdon experimented on the eggs of frogs and toads. They cloned frogs and toads by removing the nucleus from an egg and replacing it with a nucleus taken from a cell of a tadpole. However, they were unable to successfully clone a cell taken from an adult frog or toad.

These experiments fired the public's imagination. If Dolly had been born at this time, the reaction would have been very different. During the 1950s and 1960s many people thought that tinkering with life would be a boon and something to be encouraged. Few people raised concerns

During the 1950s and 1960s many scientists studied frogs' eggs, including those of the leopard frog. Frogs' eggs are large and easy to manipulate, making them good for research.

over the risks and ethics of cloning. Today, there is much more public debate and there are numerous committees that debate **ethical** issues and advise governments. Such pressure can force governments to change laws, for example to prevent scientists experimenting with human cloning.

Although Hans Spemann was the first to describe the process of cloning, he called it nuclear transplantation. The term 'clone', the Greek word for 'twig', was first used by the British biologist J.B.S. Haldane in 1963. He was speaking at a convention about the future of science, speculating on how long people would live in the future, how they would fight disease and how cloning of humans would be possible. The brightest and the best of society, he suggested, could be cloned in order to further human achievement.

'We got a good deal of reaction, both from scientists and non-scientists. They thought it was phenomenal. We thought we could clone any cell.'

Tom King, talking about the work he carried out on cloning during the 1950s

7

A change in mood

By the 1970s the mood of the public had changed. The first steps in **genetic engineering** had been made and the world's first test-tube baby was born. This involved the technique of *in vitro* **fertilization**, in which an egg is taken from a woman, fertilized in the laboratory and then replaced in the woman's **uterus** to develop into a baby. However, many people were getting worried as geneticists were achieving more complex processes and science fiction writers were publishing books on cloning which predicted that cloning could have terrible consequences. In 1978 a science writer published a book claiming that a human had been cloned. The book was presented as the 'true' story of a secret project to produce a clone of a man who had paid one million dollars to a scientist. After much debate the story was finally revealed to be a hoax. But the book was a bestseller. The book concerned both scientists and non-scientists and they did not want similar things to happen in real life.

During the 1980s, hundreds of experiments into cloning mammals failed and many leading scientists thought that it would be impossible. The breakthrough came in 1986 when sheep and cows were successfully cloned from embryo cells. However, scientists still could not successfully clone an adult cell.

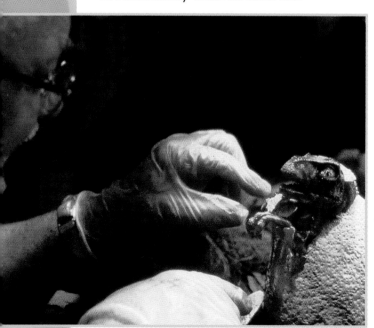

During the early 1990s, the concept of cloning was featured in many science fiction movies. The film *Blade Runner* featured human clones that were created to be drones, or workers, on other planets, but the clones revolted and returned to Earth to destroy their creators. *Jurassic Park* featured dinosaurs that were created by cloning.

In the film *Jurassic Park*, scientists had managed to reconstruct the DNA of dinosaurs. This enabled them to produce living dinosaurs.

But cloning was a real science. In 1995 a team at the Roslin Institute in Scotland, led by Ian Wilmut, had their first success when they successfully cloned two sheep called Morag and Megan. A year later Dolly was born. She was the first clone to be produced by taking a nucleus from an adult cell and placing it into an empty egg cell. The arrival of Dolly took many people, including scientists, by surprise. For years they had convinced themselves that it was impossible to make a clone of an adult cell.

'I am not a fool. I know what is bothering people about this. I understand why the world is suddenly at my door. But this is my work. It has always been my work and it doesn't have anything to do with creating copies of human beings. I am not haunted by what I do, if that is what you want to know. I sleep very well at night.'

Ian Wilmut, speaking about his work in the field of cloning and the future of human cloning

Dolly's creator

Ian Wilmut was the embryologist who produced Dolly. He had worked at Roslin Institute in Scotland for 23 years and had worked on the cloning project for ten years. The painstaking research he undertook required endless patience. He worked long hours over a microscope, studying embryonic cells. Knowing that many life-saving drugs were either difficult or expensive to produce, his aim was to create animals that could produce drugs for human use. He wanted to alter their **DNA** so that they had new **genes** to give them the ability to make a human drug. However, it was important to be able to produce many of these animals. So once an animal with new abilities had been created he needed a technique to clone it – and so his research led to the cloning of adult cells. The creation of Dolly was a huge scientific breakthrough (see pages 24–5).

Megan and Morag are identical twins. They were cloned from the same embryo that was just a few days old. The method by which they were produced was different to that which produced Dolly.

Natural cloning

This book is concerned with cloning that is carried out artificially in a laboratory. However, cloning is a process that occurs naturally, too. Cloning is used by many micro-organisms, single-celled animals and plants in order to reproduce and increase in number.

Many organisms reproduce asexually, for example bacteria, amoebae (single-celled organisms that live in water), yeast and hydras (related to the sea anemone). This means that one individual reproduces on its own without the involvement of another individual. These organisms reproduce asexually when conditions are ideal for an increase in population size, for example when there is plenty of food and space. All the new individuals are identical to the parent, so they are clones of each other. When conditions change, these organisms reproduce sexually, which involves two individuals.

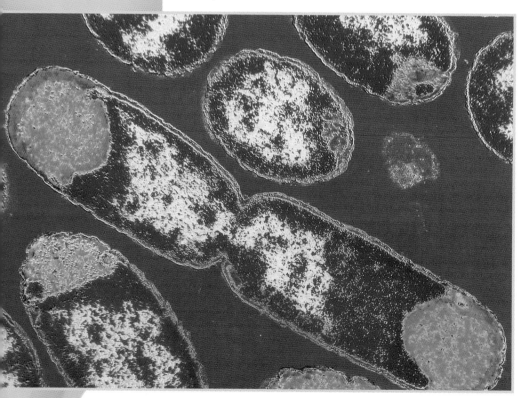

A bacterium undergoes binary fission. The cell simply divides into two. The two new daughter cells are genetically identical to each other.

Binary fission and budding

A bacterium or an amoeba can divide into two by a process called binary fission. When an amoeba is ready to reproduce, it simply splits into two. First the **nucleus** divides and then the rest of the cell. This produces two small amoebae that feed and grow. Under ideal conditions, an amoeba may divide once a day. Bacteria divide in a similar way, but they do so at a faster rate than the amoeba. Under ideal conditions, bacteria can divide every 20 minutes, so one bacterium can become one million in 7 hours.

Hydra and yeast cells reproduce asexually by budding. A hydra reproduces by growing a new hydra out of its side. At first the new bud gets its food from the parent, but eventually it is large enough to break away and live independently. Yeast is a fungus, but unlike many other types of fungi, yeast consists of single cells. When a yeast cell is large enough it produces a small outgrowth or bud which gradually gets larger. Eventually the bud breaks off to form a new cell.

Spores

Many fungi produce spores asexually. Spores are tiny spherical structures that will grow into a new individual. One such fungus is the pin mould which grows on bread and other foods. The fungus consists of a mass of tiny threads called hyphae. The hyphae grow over the surface of the food source, absorbing food. A few hyphae grow vertically and their ends become swollen. Inside, thousands of tiny spores are produced. These are released into the air where they are carried away on air currents.

Plant reproduction

Asexual reproduction occurs in plants, too. Plants such as the strawberry produce side-shoots called runners. A runner grows along the surface of the ground. Roots appear at intervals and grow into the soil. Eventually the runner between the roots withers away leaving a row of daughter plants. Grasses produce similar shoots, called tillers, while blackberries produce stolons. All of these methods are ways by which the plant can increase in number very quickly.

Potato plants reproduce asexually by producing tubers. During the summer months, the potato plant makes lots of food using **photosynthesis**. The food is moved to underground stems, which swell up and form tubers. Within the tuber the food is stored as starch. At the end of autumn the potato shoots above the ground die back, but the tubers survive underground. In spring the food in the tuber is used to fuel new growth, and each tuber begins to grow into a new plant. Since all the new plants come from the same parent, they are clones.

A strawberry plant produces a shoot called a runner, that grows along the ground. New plants form at intervals along this shoot.

Cloning plants

Plants have been cloned artificially for hundreds of years. However, the word 'cloning' is not normally used. Instead, gardeners refer to the process as 'vegetative propagation'. One example of this is when cuttings are taken. If you cut off a length of shoot from a plant and place it in a beaker of water, after a few weeks you will probably see roots appearing at the end of the shoot. Once the cutting has rooted, it can be potted into soil to grow into a new plant.

Gardeners can take cuttings of most plants in order to produce new and identical plants cheaply and quickly. Commercial companies also use vegetative propagation as it enables large numbers of identical plants to be produced in a short period of time.

New plants can be grown from seed, but seeds are produced by **sexual reproduction**. The pollen from one flower is transferred to another flower, where the male nucelus within the pollen **fertilizes** the female egg. The resulting seeds have new combinations of **genes**, so they are all different. When plants with new features are wanted, the process of sexual reproduction is useful. By crossing selected plants there is a chance that the new combination of genes will produce a plant with different features, for example a new colour of flower. But once the desired plant has been produced, the only way to produce more plants with the same features is to use vegetative propagation. This ensures that all the offspring are identical to the parent and the new feature is not lost.

Gardeners produce new plants by taking cuttings. A cutting is a short length of shoot with some of its leaves removed. The cutting is dipped in a rooting powder which stimulates the formation of roots from the bottom of the cutting.

Micropropagation

The propagation methods used commercially are slightly different to those used by gardeners, as plant companies have to produce large numbers of quality plants. One of the methods is called micropropagation or plant-tissue culture. It uses a single plant to produce a large number of clones. A short length of shoot is taken from the parent plant. This is called an explant. It is sterilized and transferred onto a jelly-like **growth medium**, which encourages the growth of shoots. The shoot that grows is divided again into many smaller pieces, each of which is grown on fresh growth medium. Then the shoots are transferred to a different medium that encourages root growth. After about four weeks the plantlets (young plants) are large enough to be potted into sterile compost.

Micropropagation has a number of advantages:
- it is quick
- it produces a large number of identical plants from one or a few parent plants
- it retains all the good features of the parental material such as colour or shape of flower, disease-resistance or high yield
- it is cost-effective
- it is easy to transport large number of plants under sterile conditions
- only healthy stock are produced
- it eliminates problems with seasonal production, as it can be carried out all year round.

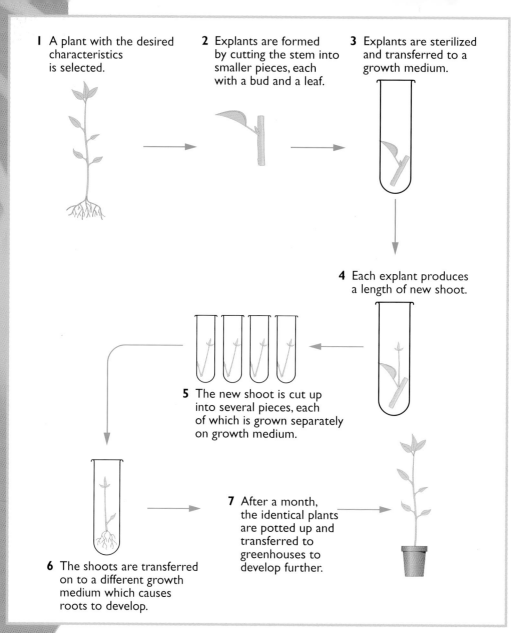

1 A plant with the desired characteristics is selected.

2 Explants are formed by cutting the stem into smaller pieces, each with a bud and a leaf.

3 Explants are sterilized and transferred to a growth medium.

4 Each explant produces a length of new shoot.

5 The new shoot is cut up into several pieces, each of which is grown separately on growth medium.

6 The shoots are transferred on to a different growth medium which causes roots to develop.

7 After a month, the identical plants are potted up and transferred to greenhouses to develop further.

This diagram shows how it is possible to produce a large number of identical plants from a single plant.

Cloning plants is a relatively straightforward process. It is possible to clone a whole plant from a single cell because every plant cell, if given the right set of conditions and chemicals, has the ability to produce unspecialized plant cells that can then be cultured to produce a whole plant.

Protoplast cloning

Improved cloning techniques mean it is now possible to clone a plant from a single cell. A small sample of tissue is removed from a plant and treated with an **enzyme** to remove the **cellulose** cell wall around each plant cell. All that is left is the protoplast – a cell without its cell wall. The protoplasts are cultured individually under sterile conditions. First they grow into a mass of unspecialized cells called a callus. Then the callus is placed on a different growth medium, which causes some of the cells to turn into roots and others to become shoots to form a tiny but complete plant.

Micropropagation units

A few botanic gardens have set up micropropagation units in order to propagate plants that are rare, **endangered** or difficult to propagate conventionally. The unit at the Royal Botanic Gardens, Kew (in London) has propagated a wide range of plants, and expertise has been developed in the micropropagation of plants that are seldom, if ever, worked on elsewhere. At any one time, approximately 500 species from all over the world are being worked on. Many of these rare and endangered species are found on islands and are particularly at risk. Projects include the propagation of rare plants from St Helena, the Mascarene Islands, Hawaii and the Canary Islands. Successful micropropagation often produces more plantlets than are required by Kew. The surplus plants are distributed to other botanic gardens around the world. Where conditions allow, some of these plants will be used in reintroduction trials – that is, attempting to return them to their country of origin. Examples of species which have been sent back include rare orchids from Sabah, Borneo and a range of plants from the Canary Islands.

The young plants in these jars have been produced by tissue culture at a micropropagation unit. They are clones of the original plant.

Chromosomes and DNA

Scientists working in the field of cloning have to have a good understanding of the role of the **genes** in the cell before they can begin their research into cloning animals.

The body needs a set of instructions to work properly. These instructions are found in almost every cell. They tell a cell what substances to make, how to grow, when to divide, and how to repair itself. In fact, they control every process that takes place in a cell. Every organism inherits these instructions from its parents. The instructions take the form of a chemical code that is located on the **chromosomes** within the **nucleus** of a cell.

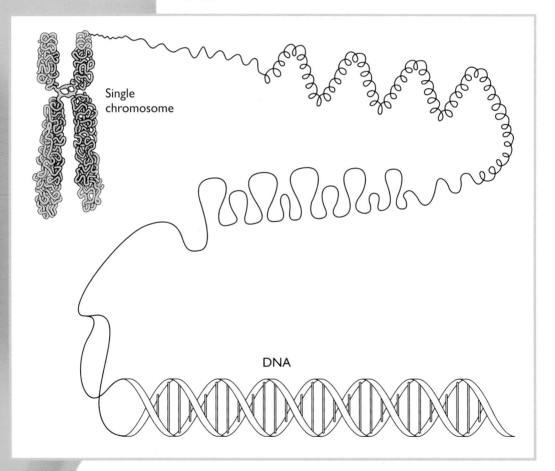

Single chromosome

DNA

This diagram shows how the long length of DNA that makes up a chromosome is tightly wound up so that the chromosome does not occupy too much space.

The make-up of chromosomes and DNA

A chromosome is a very long, thin strand made of **DNA**. The number of chromosomes in a cell is characteristic to each organism. For example, a human cell has 46 chromosomes, while a locust has 22, and a cabbage only 18.

In humans, the 46 chromosomes occur in pairs, giving a total of 23 pairs. However, human eggs and **sperm** contain only 23 chromosomes, one chromosome from each pair. At **fertilization**, a sperm fuses with an egg to form a new cell called a zygote. The combined number of chromosomes in the zygote is 46 (23 + 23). The zygote divides and becomes an **embryo**, which in turn grows into a new individual.

A chromosome is sub-divided into genes. Imagine a chromosome to be a chain of beads. Each bead represents a gene. A single chromosome can be made up of many hundreds of genes. In total, there are about 30,000 different genes carried on human chromosomes. Genes control the production of **proteins** and each gene is responsible for the production of a particular protein. So far, we only know the job of a few hundred genes but, within the very near future, scientists may know the position and role of every single one.

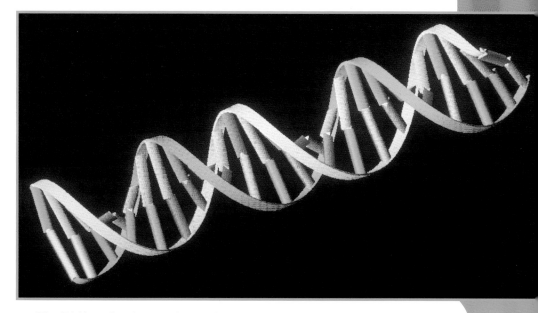

The DNA molecule is made up of two strands which twist around each other to form a double helix. The sides of the chain are made up of alternating sugar and phosphate molecules, while the rungs are formed by the bases.

DNA

A gene is a specific length of DNA on a chromosome. The letters DNA stand for deoxyribonucleic acid. DNA is a huge, coiled **molecule**. There are two strands twisted together in a spiral called a helix. It is rather like a twisted ladder, where the sides of the ladder are made from sugar and phosphate molecules. They alternate with each other: sugar – phosphate – sugar. The rungs of the ladder are formed by a link between molecules called bases. There are four different bases, adenine (A), guanine (G), cytosine (C) and thymine (T). Two of the bases, A and G, are larger than the other two. To make sure that the rungs are always the same width, A only pairs with T, and C with G.

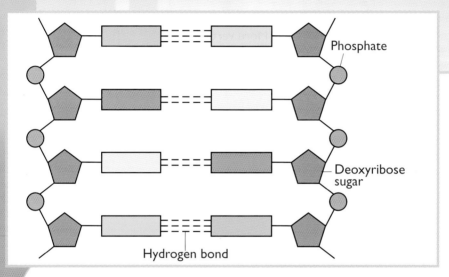

DNA is made up of sugar and phosphate molecules together with four different types of bases. The two strands of the DNA are held together by weak bonds called hydrogen bonds.

Cell specialization

As well as understanding the role of DNA within a cell, **embryologists** have to know how cells behave and how they become specialized to do a particular job.

At fertilization, a sperm fuses with an egg cell. The fertilized egg cell or zygote gains one set of genes from the father and a second set from the mother, so its genetic material is a combination of both parents' genes. The zygote starts to undergo cell division and becomes an embryo, which develops into a new individual. Every cell in the body of this new individual arises from the same fertilized egg and this means that every cell has the same set of genes.

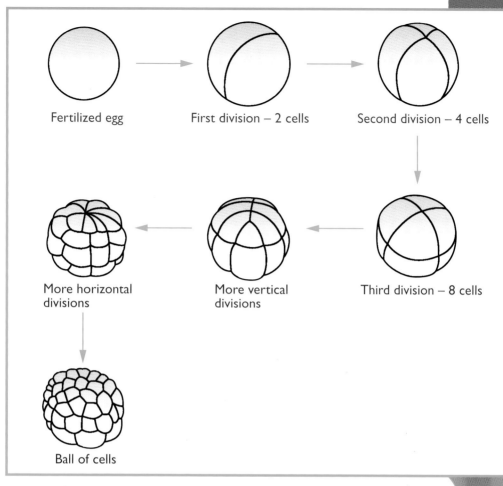

Fertilized egg

First division – 2 cells

Second division – 4 cells

Third division – 8 cells

More vertical divisions

More horizontal divisions

Ball of cells

The single cell of the zygote undergoes many divisions to form a ball of cells. Once the embryo has reached the eight-cell stage, the individual cells start to differentiate (become different).

Differentiation

The zygote divides to form two cells, each of which divides to form two cells, making four cells in all. Each cell then divides and divides again. Soon there is a hollow ball of cells. At this stage all the cells are the same. After about fourteen days, the cells start to take on a different appearance. Their structure changes in order to carry out different jobs, for example there are nerve cells, skin cells, liver cells and so on. This process of specialization is called differentiation. Eventually there will be hundreds of different types of cell, each specialized to carry out a particular job.

Once a cell has reached its final form, its appearance will not alter. So although the genes in a liver cell and a nerve cell are the same, the cells look very different and have different jobs.

Switching genes on and off

The DNA in an unspecialized cell is the same as the DNA in a specialized one. However, during the process of cell specialization, some of the genes are switched off, while others are left on. The active genes are those that are required for the cell's specialized functions. Any genes that are not required are switched off. So, a nerve cell has a different set of active genes to a liver cell.

A term that is used a lot in **genetics** is 'gene expression'. It refers to a gene being switched on and able to have an effect or express itself. Many hormones and drugs work by switching on or off particular genes in the body in order to control the production of a particular protein by that gene.

One of the biggest challenges for embryologists is to take a specialized cell such as a liver cell and return the cell to an unspecialized condition with all its genes switched on (see page 22).

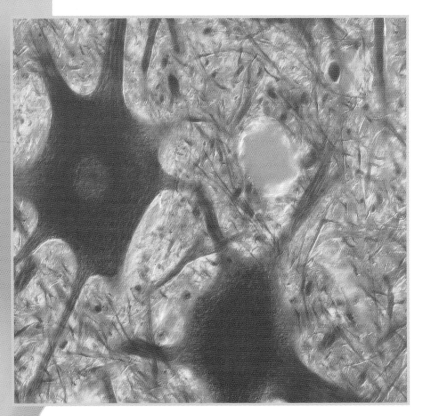

A mass of nerve cells in the brain. A nerve cell is specialized to carry out the specific job of sending electrical impulses from one nerve cell to another.

Human Genome Project

The Human Genome Project was one of the most ambitious biological projects ever undertaken. It was started in 1990 with teams of scientists from all around the world taking part. Its aim was to discover the sequence of bases that make up all the genes in human DNA, the genome being the complete set of genetic information contained within a cell. It was not an easy task, for our genes only make up five per cent of the DNA. They are separated by long lengths of non-functional DNA – nicknamed 'junk' DNA. In 2001 the first draft of the human **genetic code** was published. However, there is still some way to go before the information can be used effectively. The information produced by this project could be compared with a dictionary of a foreign language. It is almost impossible to generate meaningful sentences in this language simply by using the human genome dictionary. The next stage is to understand which combination of words – or co-expressed genes – are important to biological processes.

Dr John Sulston is director of the Sanger Centre near Cambridge, UK. This research institute is one of the many that has been involved with the Human Genome Project.

Cloning in the lab

Cloning plants is relatively simple but cloning animals, especially mammals, is far more complex. Think about a plant cutting. The new cells that form at the end of the cutting, if given the right chemicals, will develop into root cells. The same is not true of most animals. If a person's arm is cut off, it will not sprout a new body. Once an animal cell has become specialized, it cannot revert to being unspecialized. So scientists working with animal cloning have to work out how they can transfer the genetic material of a specialized cell into an unspecialized cell and then switch on all of its **genes**.

Specialized cells

A human body contains hundreds of different kinds of cell, and there are billions of each kind. A liver cell has one set of active genes, while a muscle cell has another. This is what makes the cells different. In the previous chapter you read about how the cells become specialized. The critical stage is when the **embryo** becomes a ball of eight cells. It is at this stage that the process of change begins, a change that cannot be reversed.

Embryologists have discovered that any cell removed from the embryo up to the eight-cell stage has the ability to survive on its own and to continue to divide to form a new, but identical, individual. It has all the genetic information required to produce the whole range of cell types. It is the same process that occurs when identical twins are produced. In fact, embryologists have produced identical quintuplet sheep from five of the eight cells of an eight-cell sheep embryo. The technique is relatively simple – the cells are carefully pulled apart, allowed to grow and then placed in the **uterus** of a **surrogate** mother. After the eight-cell stage, the cells lose their ability to produce all the different tissues that make up a complete organism.

Methods of cloning

There are two main methods of animal cloning, embryo cloning and **nuclear transfer**. So far, most animal clones have been produced using embryo cloning. In this method, the embryos produced are not identical to either parents as there is a mix of genes from both parents (see panel on page 23).

Embryo cloning

The method of cloning a cow using the technique of embryo cloning is as follows:

1 A sample of **sperm** is taken from a bull with the desired features.
2 The sample is placed in a glass Petri dish that contains an egg taken from a cow.
3 *In vitro* **fertilization** occurs.
4 The single fertilized cell divides to form two cells, which divide again to form four cells and then a ball of eight cells.
5 The tiny embryo is carefully split up to form more embryos. Each of these embryos is identical – they are clones of each other. However, unlike in plant cloning, the embryos are not identical to either parent as there is a mix of genes from both parents.
6 Each embryo is transferred into the uterus of a cow, which becomes a surrogate.

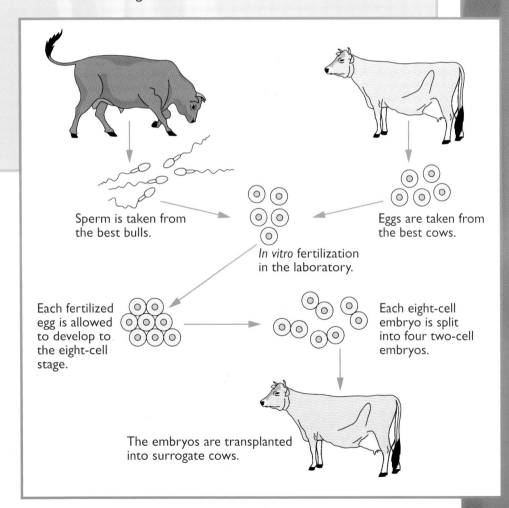

Sperm is taken from the best bulls.

Eggs are taken from the best cows.

In vitro fertilization in the laboratory.

Each fertilized egg is allowed to develop to the eight-cell stage.

Each eight-cell embryo is split into four two-cell embryos.

The embryos are transplanted into surrogate cows.

Cloning by nuclear transfer

The nuclear transfer method was used to create Dolly (see panel on page 25). This is different to embryo cloning as it produces a clone that is identical to its parent. It is a method that can be used to recreate animals with useful characteristics, perhaps cows that have a high milk-yield or chickens that lay large numbers of eggs. By cloning the animals, none of their desirable features will be lost. Instead, they will be retained – not diluted by the mixing that would otherwise occur with another set of genes from another parent.

Poor hit rate

Cloning does not have a high success rate. When you read how Dolly was created it all sounds very straightforward. But the process was incredibly difficult and there were many failures. The research team tried the process of fusing the udder cell with an egg cell 277 times, and only obtained 29 embryos. The embryos were grown for a week and then placed in different surrogate sheep, but only one lamb, Dolly, was born.

Many cloned animals are born sickly, or unusually large and many do not live long. It is possible that this is due to tiny changes to the genes. This affects the production of **proteins**, which are essential to the animal's survival. In the future, scientists may be able to screen the cloned embryos so they can destroy any faulty ones.

> 'There have been reports of high mortality in cloned cows and sheep. Clones have died hours or days after delivery or had abnormally high birth weights.'
>
> Philip Damiani, research scientist, Advanced Cell Technology

Old DNA

There is concern that a newly born clone would have **DNA** that was as old as the parent cell. For example, Dolly was born with the same DNA as that of her mother, a six-year-old ewe. Nobody is sure what effect this could have, but theoretically it could reduce the life span of the cloned animal. Some scientists have commented on the fact that cloned animals have bits missing from the end of their **chromosomes**. Dolly has led a healthy life so far, but only time will tell if her lifespan is shorter than normal.

How was Dolly created?

Dolly's mother was a six-year-old Finn Dorset ewe. Cells were taken from her udder and grown for a week in a low-nutrient **growth medium**. This medium kept the cells alive, but stopped them dividing. Then an unfertilized egg was removed from a Scottish Blackface ewe. The **nucleus**, containing the DNA, was sucked out. One of the **donor** sheep's udder cells was slipped under the outer membrane of the egg. A tiny burst of electricity was passed through them, causing the donor cell to fuse with the egg cell. Now the egg cell had a new nucleus – the nucleus of the udder cell. A second burst of electricity jump-started the cell into dividing. Soon there was a ball of cells. This was allowed to grow for a week before being transferred into the uterus of another Scottish Blackface ewe. The embryo continued to develop and 148 days later Dolly was born. Although Dolly was born to a black-faced ewe, she was identical to her real mother, the Finn Dorset ewe.

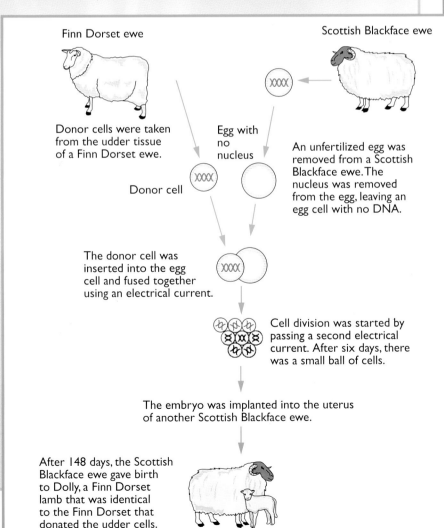

Finn Dorset ewe

Scottish Blackface ewe

Donor cells were taken from the udder tissue of a Finn Dorset ewe.

Egg with no nucleus

An unfertilized egg was removed from a Scottish Blackface ewe. The nucleus was removed from the egg, leaving an egg cell with no DNA.

Donor cell

The donor cell was inserted into the egg cell and fused together using an electrical current.

Cell division was started by passing a second electrical current. After six days, there was a small ball of cells.

The embryo was implanted into the uterus of another Scottish Blackface ewe.

After 148 days, the Scottish Blackface ewe gave birth to Dolly, a Finn Dorset lamb that was identical to the Finn Dorset that donated the udder cells.

Cloning in action

Although the techniques of cloning are far from perfect, enough is known for scientists to make use of them in other research projects. Cloning will allow scientists to manufacture drugs in new ways and to improve livestock such as chickens, sheep and cows.

Living drugs factory

Many drugs are difficult and expensive to make and a single dose can cost hundreds of pounds. This means that their use has to be limited. **Genetic engineering** and cloning offer a way of changing the genetic make-up of an animal so that it can make the drug. For example, a cow or a sheep may be genetically engineered so that the female produces a particular drug, usually in the form of a **protein**, in her milk. The protein is then extracted from the milk. Proteins can be difficult to create in the laboratory, so using animals to produce the protein is an effective way of producing large quantities of a pure product.

The first of these genetically engineered animals was a sheep that made a human protein called alpha-1 antitrypsin, which is used to treat an inherited lung disease. The method used was very unpredictable. Scientists removed the **gene** that was responsible for making the protein from human **DNA** and injected it into sheep **embryos**. They did this to thousands of embryos in the hope that a few would take up the gene and be able to make the protein. The first sheep that were born were called Megan and Morag (see page 9). However, these sheep cannot be allowed to reproduce in the normal way as the ability to produce the protein may be lost. If more sheep are required, the scientists either have to repeat the method of inserting the gene into embryos or find a way of cloning the engineered sheep. In fact, the research behind the creation of Dolly was aimed at finding a way of cloning genetically engineered sheep such as Megan and Morag. There is now another cloned sheep at the Roslin Institute. Her name is Polly and she has had a human gene inserted into her DNA so that she can produce milk that contains human Factor IX. This is a blood-clotting agent needed by people with haemophilia, a disease in which this agent is missing.

Genetically engineered chickens

Chickens too have been genetically altered to produce useful drugs. Research companies in the USA have produced chickens that have anti-cancer drugs in their eggs. The first anti-cancer bird produced was called Alvin. Other birds have been produced that make human growth factor and human **antibodies**. The yield of drugs from these genetically engineered chickens could be large and lucrative. Hens produce as many as 300 eggs per year, each of which could contain up to 100 milligrams of a drug.

In the future, genetically engineered hens could produce eggs that contain drugs needed to treat humans. Extraction of the drug from the egg would be a relatively straightforward process.

Cloned farm animals

Cloning offers a way for farmers to improve their stock over a short period of time. At present, most farmers use the lengthy process of selective breeding to improve their stock. They choose animals with desirable characteristics to be parents of the new generation of animals. **Artificial insemination** can help. **Semen** is taken from male animals that show desirable characteristics. This is frozen and stored for future use. Farmers can purchase the semen and use it to **fertilize** their own animals. However, this process is not reliable and it may take several generations before the desirable characteristics are produced.

Farmers regularly use the method of artificial insemination to fertilize their cows. This means that they can use the semen taken from a bull with desirable characteristics. Semen from the best bulls may be used to fertilize hundreds of cows worldwide.

Clones of Zita

In 1997, a dairy cow named Zita was the highest ranked Holstein cow in the USA. She produced almost 18,000 litres of milk, with 5.1 per cent butterfat, almost double the national average. Her daughters and granddaughters have proved to be just as productive. Zita was the ideal cow to clone. Tissue samples were taken of Zita and stored for future use. In March 2001, cloned calves of Zita were born and they should be just as productive as the original Zita. More clones are planned of both Zita and other high ranking cows and bulls.

Cows only produce one calf at a time, so a few farmers are using embryo cloning to produce larger numbers of calves. The parents are carefully chosen and the embryo they produce is split to produce many identical copies. Each of the clones is placed into a **surrogate** mother. Although more calves are produced, none is identical to either of the parents. Greater improvements will be made once cloning by **nuclear transfer** becomes more commonplace. In the future, farmers may be able to buy embryos that are clones of the most productive cows of the best herds. This method has the potential to lift the performance of a farmer's herd to that of the very best within one or two generations. It is likely that specialist companies would sell cloned embryos in much the same way as they now sell semen. Farmers would choose cloned embryos from catalogues that described the animal's traits, such as fertility (ability to produce offspring), health and long-term performance. Then the cloned embryo would be delivered to the farm for implanting into one of the farmer's own cows.

> 'The moral issues raised by cloning are neither large nor more profound than the questions human beings have already faced in regard to such technologies as nuclear energy, **recombinant DNA** and computer **encryption**. They are simply new.'
>
> From an open letter written by the International Academy of Humanists in 1997, the signatories include Francis Crick (who, with James Watson, discovered the structure of DNA) and Richard Dawkins (Professor of the Public Understanding of Science at Oxford University and author of the book *The Selfish Gene*)

Spare-part surgery

One of the most exciting developments of cloning is in the field of medical research. It is already possible to grow skin cells in the laboratory for repairing burnt skin. But cloning may allow doctors to produce a never-ending supply of organs for **transplant** operations.

Cloning for medical treatments

Bone marrow is a liquid-like tissue found in the centre of the body's largest bones. It is the site of formation of red blood cells (which carry oxygen around the body), white blood cells (involved in the defence against disease) and platelets (which help the blood to clot). Because bone marrow has no fixed shape or form it is considered to be the easiest tissue to clone.

Patients who contract **leukaemia** produce too many white blood cells in their blood – the cells multiply out of control. One of the best chances of beating this cancer is for the patient to have their own bone marrow destroyed and replaced with healthy bone marrow from a **donor**. But it is difficult to find a donor with bone marrow that has the right blood type to match the patient – if the bone marrow does not match, the body rejects it. Many people die before a suitable donor is found.

The bone marrow is one of the most important tissues in the body, since it is the site of the formation of new red blood cells, some white blood cells and platelets.

Cloning could change this. The treatment would involve taking a patient's cell and fusing it with an egg cell that has had its **nucleus** removed. The egg with its new **genes** would start to divide. The critical step would be the addition of chemicals that instruct the cells to become bone marrow cells. If successful, this technique would produce bone marrow cells that were identical to the patient's own bone marrow and there would be no chance of rejection.

Treating bone marrow cancer

Patients with bone marrow cancer often need heavy doses of anti-tumour drugs. (A tumour is an abnormal growth of cells.) Unfortunately these drugs often kill off healthy bone marrow cells, which are unaffected by the cancer, as well as diseased ones. A possible new treatment involves the removal of the healthy cells. These cells are then grown in the lab and **genetically engineered**. This involves introducing a gene that gives them resistance against the anti-tumour drug. The engineered cells are injected back into the patient's bone marrow where they multiply. Then the patient is given the drug. Because the healthy bone marrow cells are resistant to the drugs, large doses can be given to kill off the cancer cells. This treatment could increase the patient's chances of survival and making a full recovery.

Artificial skin

An artificial skin can now be produced from cloned cells to treat patients suffering from burns. Skin that has been badly burnt needs to be covered to keep it clean, prevent infections and minimize scarring. Sometimes, if the skin is too badly damaged to repair itself, a skin graft is required. This involves removing healthy skin from another part of the body and attaching it to the damaged area. Skin is also available from tissue banks, but donated skin can be problematic as it sometimes causes infection and the body may reject it. There are 2,000,000 serious burn victims in the USA each year and of these, 15,000 need skin grafts. The US Red Cross estimates that only one-sixth of the skin needed for burn victims is available from the nation's tissue banks. Skin is taken from organ donors after they die, but it can cost as much as $1000 for 30 cm^2, and comes in thin strips that must be pieced together like a patchwork quilt. It may also harbour viruses including **HIV**. Artificial skin is beginning to help the situation.

The process of making artificial skin starts with a soupy mixture of skin cells that is pumped on to an ultra-thin plastic mesh. Within a week, the cells have multiplied and filled the mesh to produce a layer of skin. This is then frozen until needed. Then the surgeon unfreezes the patch and stretches it over the burn site. It is left there until the patient is ready for a graft. At the moment this artificial skin is only temporary, but it allows the patient's own skin to heal until it is ready for a skin graft. In the future it may be possible to develop a permanent skin, which would mean that skin grafts were no longer required.

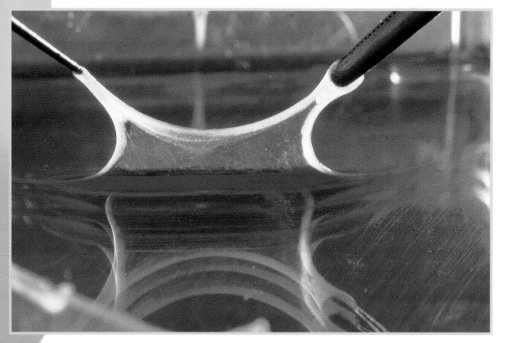

A layer of new skin cells is carefully removed from a culture solution. It can be used to treat the skin of people who have suffered severe burns.

Organs for transplants

Tragically for many people, there is a shortage of organs for transplant patients. There are far more people on the waiting lists to receive a transplant that there are donors. Many patients die or suffer prolonged periods of illness as a result. Even when organs are available there are problems with transplantation. The major problem, whether of whole organs or just a few cells, is rejection. The body of the patient identifies the transplant as being foreign and starts to attack it.

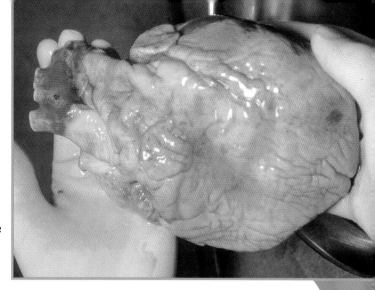

Basically, the human body's **immune system** is designed to attack anything it considers foreign in order to protect the body from disease. Unfortunately, however, it can't tell the difference between unwanted foreign bodies and desirable ones such as a transplanted organ. Normally, a transplant patient is treated with immuno-suppressant drugs, which stop the body's immune system

This heart is ready to be placed into the chest of a transplant patient. However, the patient will have to receive immuno-suppressant drugs to stop rejection.

from attacking the organ, but this leaves them vulnerable to disease. In addition, the patient has to take the drugs for life to stop any rejection. Some patients, despite receiving the drugs, still reject the new organ.

Cloning could help transplant patients. There are three possible ways forward:
- to breed animals specially for organ donation
- to build new hearts, kidneys, livers and so on in the laboratory
- to use **stem cells**.

Xenotransplantation

Animals, such as pigs, may be used as a source of organs. When animal organs are used, the process is known as xenotransplantation. Pigs are the most likely donors, as their organs are the most compatible with humans and they are easy to raise. However, the **proteins** on the surface of their organs are very different to our own, so a human body would normally recognize them as being foreign and therefore reject them. One way around this problem is to genetically engineer the pig so that its organs would not be rejected when transplanted into a human. Scientists have identified a particular signal on the cells of human organs that, if present on pig cells, would prevent rejection. The gene that makes this protein has been identified and inserted into the **DNA** of a pig. This pig has been bred and there is now a small herd of pigs available for xenotransplantation in clinical trials. Unfortunately, pigs carry a number of viruses that could affect the human body and it is considered unlikely that it will be possible to breed virus-free pigs.

Animals such as pigs could be bred specifically as organ donors. However, this raises many **ethical** and moral problems.

Xenotransplantation issues

Raising genetically engineered pigs purely for organ donation raises many issues. First, is it right to alter an animal in such a way that it can be used for organ transplantation? It could be argued that we raise animals for many purposes already, including food and leather. Pigs altered for the purposes of organ donation would have to be very well looked after – kept in clean housing and well fed – in order to ensure that the organs were of top quality. But what about the actual use of an animal organ to replace a diseased one in a human body? Many people feel uncomfortable about this idea. However, imagine you had an incurable heart disease and the only chance of survival was to have your diseased heart replaced by a healthy pig's heart? Perhaps given that choice you would happily agree. Some people would strongly object on religious grounds. Many people consider pigs to be unclean animals and they do not eat pork or other food derived from pigs. These people would consider this development an unacceptable medical option.

Building whole organs

The second approach – making artificial organs – is still at the early stages of development. Already teams have successfully grown tissues such as skin and cartilage. Patients have had cartilage cells removed from damaged knee joints and grown in the laboratory before being transplanted back into the knee. However, there are ambitious plans to grow hearts, livers and kidneys (see page 49).

Stem cells

Much research at the moment is centred on a particular type of cell called a stem cell. These cells are specialized, but unlike other specialized cells, they can divide to make more cells. In addition, they have the ability to create other specialized cell types as they multiply. Stem cells occur at all stages of development, from the **embryo** to the adult, but their versatility and numbers decrease with age. An embryonic stem cell has the ability to produce any one of the 200 different specialized cell types in the body, but an adult stem cell can only make a few.

It is the stem cell's ability to create other cell types that interests scientists. Tissues such as skin, intestines and blood undergo continual cell replacement. As some cells die, others are produced to replace them. The stem cells in these tissues continually divide to provide the replacement cells. Other types of tissue have a few stem cells that are non-active until the tissue is damaged. If damage occurs, for example to muscle tissue, the stem cells start to divide again to repair the damage. However, many tissues do not have any stem cells, so the specialized cells cannot be replaced if they are damaged. For example, a person is born with millions of nerve cells in the brain. Each day some of these cells die and they are not replaced. Sometimes diseased or damaged cells can be replaced by organ transplantation.

Soon, it may be possible to treat patients by transplanting specialized cells that have been grown from stem cells in the laboratory. This is called cell replacement therapy. Patients suffering from extensive burns, leukaemia, as well as degenerative diseases – of the brain (**Parkinson's** disease), pancreas (diabetes), liver (hepatitis), joints (rheumatoid arthritis), heart and kidneys – would all benefit from cell replacement therapy. Damaged organs or tissues could be injected with healthy normal cells. When given the correct signal, these cells regenerate the tissue around them and even produce new cells to replace those that have been damaged or killed.

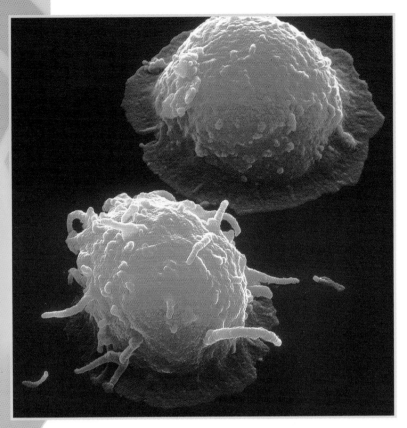

These are stem cells in the umbilical cord of a baby. Harvesting stem cells raises fewer ethical objections than using cells from a developing embryo.

Embryonic stem cells

The best stem cells to work on are those taken from embryos that are about one week old. An embryo at this stage in its development is about the size of a full stop and is made up of about 100 cells. Scientists can take a few of these cells and grow them for many weeks, so that they multiply to make many more stem cells. Once there are enough cells present, they can be treated in such a way as to start the process of cell specialization.

Scientists can use stem cells taken from adults, but these stem cells only grow for a short period of time, so fewer can be produced and they cannot make as many types of cell, so overall they are far less useful.

Preventing rejection

If the cells produced from stem cells were simply injected into the body, they too would be rejected, just like a transplanted organ. However, rejection can be avoided by cloning the cells. The ideal method of treatment would be to take some stem cells from the patient and culture them in the laboratory in order to produce a supply of specialized cells that could be placed back inside the patient's body. Since the cells came from the patient, there would be no rejection. However, as adults only have a few stem cells with limited potential, the alternative approach is nuclear replacement. In this method, an embryonic cell has its nucleus removed and replaced with a nucleus taken from a cell of the patient. The cloned cell would grow into stem cells that would be used to make the specialized cells for transplant.

Cloning cells for the treatment of medical conditions is called **therapeutic cloning**, and it is regulated by laws. In the UK, only approved research laboratories can carry out cloning on human embryos and the embryos must not be more than fourteen days old. The issues concerned with research on human embryos is explored fully in the next chapter. Even if therapeutic cloning was to become feasible it would be a very expensive treatment. Most patients would not be able to afford such treatments and it would be restricted to a few who could afford the treatments offered by private clinics.

Cloning adult cells

Eventually, it may be possible to reprogram adult cells so that they revert to being stem cells. In November 1998, an American company called Advanced Cell Technology (see page 54) successfully cloned human cells using the technique of **nuclear transfer**, similar to that used to produce Dolly. An egg was taken from a cow and its nucleus removed. This left an 'empty' cell into which DNA, taken from a human leg cell, was placed. The cell was treated in such a way as to make it start behaving like a new embryo, so it started to divide. This 'embryo' was allowed to develop for twelve days before being destroyed. This research is aimed at producing human stem cells. There is still much work to be done, but this is a promising option as it does not involve the use of human embryos.

Human cloning

Human cloning is at the heart of the cloning debate. It is probably the one area of cloning that people have the most concern about. Ask somebody about human cloning and they will probably think of Frankenstein's monster or have visions of people emerging from vats where they have been grown – all the stuff of science fiction books and movies. How far have the scientists come along the road to this vision of the future?

In this chapter we will look at the issues associated with human **reproductive cloning**. This is very different to the **therapeutic cloning** described in the previous chapter, where the **embryos** used in the research process are not allowed to grow for more than fourteen days. Reproductive cloning would involve the creation of a second, genetically identical human being using the **nucleus** of a presently living person. This would be done by replacing the nucleus of a human egg cell with the nucleus from an adult cell. The modified embryo would then be implanted in a woman's **uterus** where it would develop into a new individual. It is important to remember that, unlike therapeutic cloning methods, the methods discussed in this chapter are theoretical. As yet, human reproductive cloning is not allowed in any country.

In vitro fertilization (IVF)

The first step on the road to human cloning started with the first test-tube baby in 1978. This made use of a revolutionary technique in which a human egg was **fertilized** outside the body. Nowadays this technique, called *in vitro* **fertilization** or IVF, is carried out routinely on **infertile** women. The infertility is often caused by blocked Fallopian tubes, which lead from the woman's ovaries (where her eggs are stored). Fertilization normally takes place in one of the tubes. IVF treatment involves removing some of the woman's eggs from her ovaries and fertilizing them externally. The resulting embryo is returned to her uterus so pregnancy can proceed as normal.

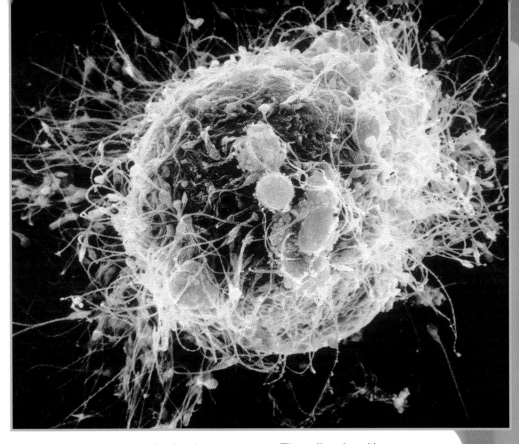

A newly fertilized egg or zygote. The yellow hair-like structures are sperm still attached to it. After *in vitro* fertilization, this cell is cultured in the laboratory until it has grown into a ball of eight cells. Then it is placed in the mother's uterus.

Test-tube babies

The first stage in IVF treatment is hormone treatment to stimulate the woman's ovaries into producing many eggs. The eggs are collected by inserting a hollow needle through the wall of the vagina (the passageway leading to the uterus). They are placed in a fluid that is similar to that which exists in the Fallopian tubes. Healthy **sperm** are added to the fluid and fertilization takes place. The fertilized egg cells are grown until they reach the four- to eight-cell embryo stage. The embryos are examined to make sure they are healthy and then two or three are implanted in the uterus. By implanting more than one there is a greater chance of success. Occasionally, all three survive and the woman gives birth to triplets. Any unused embryos can be stored at ⁻173 °C in case the first attempt is unsuccessful. Sometimes, women may give permission for any spare embryos to be used for research.

Helping infertility

A lot of research into human infertility is taking place. However, even more could be done if doctors were allowed to use cloning techniques. Some fertility clinics are pushing for the rules on human reproductive cloning to be relaxed so that they can treat infertile couples more successfully. In the UK, the creation, use and storage of human embryos outside the body is controlled by the Human Fertilisation and Embryology Authority. This authority has very strict rules by which all fertility clinics must operate. In addition, all fertility clinics need a licence issued by this authority. Currently, it is illegal to carry out research on a human embryo more than fourteen days old. Any embryo used for research must not be replaced in a uterus. It is also illegal to produce identical individuals, or clones, by substituting the nucleus in an embryonic cell with one taken from another human. Embryos may not be produced by combining the eggs or sperm of humans with those of animals. Infertility is a very emotional topic. A lot of childless couples feel that their lives are incomplete without children. The desire of a wealthy, childless couple to have a child at almost any cost could mean that they may persuade a fertility clinic to help them, even if it is illegal.

In the future, it is possible that the rules will be relaxed to help infertile couples have children. This could mean that the cloning of early embryo cells will be allowed. The process mimics the natural process that results in identical twins. Sometimes, an embryo splits

Identical twins are formed when a young embryo splits into two to form two separate individuals.

into two and the two parts continue to develop normally, creating identical twins or even triplets. Doctors would recreate this in the laboratory. An embryo would be produced by IVF. Then the cells of the early embryo would be separated to make several identical embryos or clones (the same procedure described on page 23). One would be implanted in the woman's uterus, the rest frozen for future attempts. This way a woman could end up with identical twins or triplets, but they would be born several years apart.

The advantages of cloning

What are the advantages of producing clones of a single embryo? IVF treatment is very painful for the woman and is not without risk. It would be safer and cheaper for the laboratory to take one egg, fertilize it and then split it to create many embryos. These embryos would develop into individuals who were identical to each other, but different from their parents. Any woman who could not produce healthy eggs or had stopped producing eggs could use eggs from a **donor**. The nucleus would be removed from the donor egg and replaced with **DNA** from either the woman or her partner. This way the child would be a clone of one its parents.

There are some procedures that could help women who miscarry (lose their baby during the pregnancy). One of the causes of a miscarriage is faulty **cytoplasm** in the cells of the embryo. This problem could be overcome by using a cloning technique. First, a fertilized egg cell would be produced using IVF. The nucleus of this cell would be removed and placed inside an empty donor egg with a healthy cytoplasm. This means that the genetic material would come from the mother and father, but would be present in a cell with healthy cytoplasm, so the woman would not miscarry.

Welfare concerns

Many people are not opposed to the process of embryo cloning, but they are very concerned about the welfare of the children that are born as a result of this process. Ian Wilmut, the creator of Dolly (see page 9), was asked whether he was opposed to multiple embryos. He replied that he did not object to the process, but only if all the embryos were used at the same time, so the mother gave birth to identical twins or triplets. He did not like the idea of freezing surplus embryos for use at a future date. His fear was that a newborn baby would be a clone of an older child. The older child would have already developed its own identity. Because the younger child had an identical appearance, it might not be treated as a unique individual.

Is cloning safer than sex?

Some scientists argue that cloning is safer than **sexual reproduction**. The fertilization process is not 100 per cent perfect. One of the most common causes of human birth defects is having too few or too many **chromosomes**. The chances of a chromosome abnormality increases with age, especially in mothers over the age of 40. If there is a serious defect the embryo does not survive. A few survive a while longer but die between weeks nine and twelve, and then the mother suffers a miscarriage. However, a small percentage will be born.

The most common chromosome disorder is having one chromosome too many – for example, the condition Downs Syndrome is caused by the presence of an extra copy of one small chromosome. These chromosome disorders would not happen with cloning, as only healthy cells with the correct number of chromosomes would be used. Some babies are born with genetic disorders such as cystic fibrosis and sickle-cell anaemia. Cloning would prevent this too, since the cloned cells would be screened to make sure that they do not have any genetic defects.

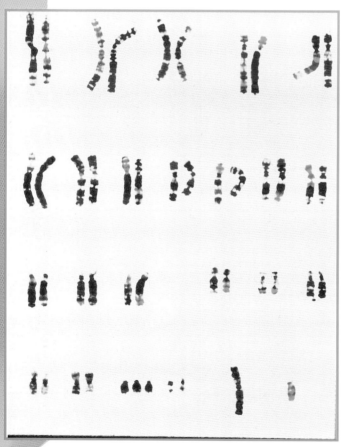

If you look carefully at this photograph of chromosomes taken from a person with Downs Syndrome, you will see that there are 47 chromosomes, instead of 46. Normally there are two copies of each chromosome. But this individual has three of chromosome number 22 (bottom row of chromosomes).

Donor clones

There is a worry that human clones could be produced with the sole intent of using them as donors. The clone could be used as a donor in a number of ways. Parents who have a child suffering from a life-threatening illness such as **leukaemia** could decide to clone the child in order to create an identical child who would be the perfect **bone marrow** donor. There is a possibility that people would create donors solely with the intention of using the clone as a source of **transplant** organs. For example, a wealthy person could pay to have a clone of him or herself created, in order to use their heart to replace their own diseased heart. It sounds ruthless, but there are no doubt people who would pay large sums of money to extend their own lifespans. These **ethical** issues have to be debated in public and, if necessary, laws have to be passed to regulate human cloning.

Is human cloning realistic?

There are many practical reasons why human cloning is not carried out at the moment. During the research that went into creating Dolly, more than 400 unfertilized eggs were taken from donor ewes. Human IVF clinics recover an average of five to ten eggs at a time from each woman donor. This means that any clinic wanting to work in human cloning would need to recruit at least 40 volunteers for each prospective pregnancy. The actual number of eggs needed would be much greater than this, since there is less than a one in five chance of become pregnant following IVF. These figures suggest that the chances of establishing a successful pregnancy from a cloned human embryo are between three and ten times lower than in sheep. During the experiments to produce Dolly, hundreds of embryos died. The same would happen with human embryos.

Who might do the cloning?

Although human cloning is banned in most countries of the world, there is a strong possibility that somebody somewhere will carry it out. The most likely place for this to happen is a fertility clinic. Fertility clinics have doctors with expertise in removing eggs from women, carrying out the *in vitro* fertilization and replacing the embryos in the uterus. Such expertise is not found in biotechnology companies and research laboratories. In addition, the would-be cloners need women who are willing to donate eggs. Again, fertility clinics have this access. It is even possible that human cloning has already taken place. Unless a clinic made the information public, nobody would be any the wiser.

Risks of cloning

Cloning is still in its infancy and the technology is still relatively crude. Many clones have abnormalities that cause them to die during pregnancy or soon after being born. Until these problems are overcome, most scientists believe it is not right for anyone to carry out experiments in humans that could result in a malformed child. Even if a cloned baby appeared to be normal, he or she could have hidden abnormalities. When adult cells are used to create a clone, mutations (changes in genetic material) can be transferred with them. For example, the resulting clone could have a shortened lifespan or increased chance of cancer later in life, or one of thousands of other defects. Experience with cloning in farm animals may identify ways of reducing risk but this is likely to take many years.

The debate about human embryo research

The issue of human embryo research is surrounded by controversy. It continues to be debated by scientists and non-scientists and by governments. The human embryos used for research into therapeutic cloning can grow until they are fourteen days old and must then be destroyed. Those people who support this research argue that the embryos have been produced by artificial fertilization in a laboratory. The embryo is just a ball of cells that could not survive outside of the body. However, other people, especially pro-life supporters (anti-abortionists), do not agree with using human embryos. They believe that all embryos have the potential to develop into a new individual and do not want any form of human embryo research. By destroying the embryos at fourteen days, they say, researchers are killing a potential individual. They are also concerned that this research brings human cloning one step nearer.

Why fourteen days?

Research on embryos in the UK is only permitted for fourteen days following fertilization. Up until fourteen days the embryo consists of a collection of dividing cells which are loosely clustered together. None of the cells have started to specialize. At fourteen days a change takes place – a groove appears on the upper side of the embryo. This is called the primitive streak. This marks the stage that the cells start to specialize. At this point experimentation has to stop and the embryos have to be destroyed.

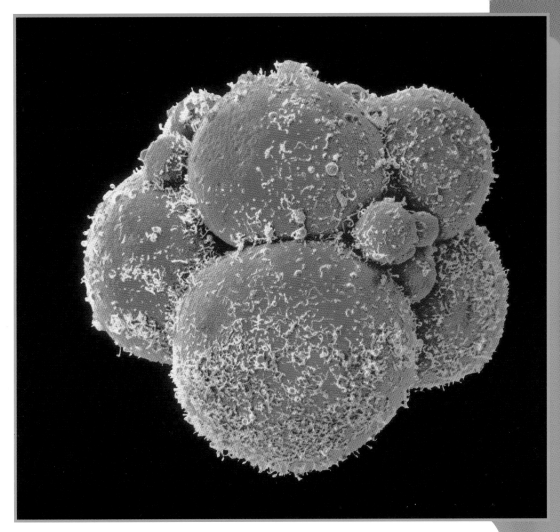

This embryo is at the eight-cell stage and the cells are identical and undifferentiated. Research can be carried out on this embryo until it is fourteen days old.

Drawing the line

Many countries have implemented a temporary ban on all research using human embryos until the matter can be thoroughly debated. So what would happen if the ban became permanent? Most importantly, it would stop research into potentially life-saving medical procedures – for example, the growing of organs for transplant operations. Would people want to give up this possibility? If you were dying from heart disease would you want the opportunity to clone your heart for your own survival? So perhaps limited research into human cloning is all right.

The difficulty lies in where to draw the line. When does research into life-saving medical procedures stop and creating a baby that is a clone start? What about childless couples who are desperate for a baby? Is it okay to allow research into infertility? Would it be okay to clone a human from a cell taken from an early embryo rather than from a cell of a living adult?

Answering these questions is difficult. Some people argue that if we really want to stop the possibility of human cloning we must stop all research. This would be regardless of the benefits to human health, as any research in this area would form the first few steps towards human clones. Quite rightly, there are many laws controlling research into human embryos. In 2001, after considerable debate, the UK government allowed further research into human embryos to take place. After considering all the evidence, the government decided that the benefits from this type of research outweighed the risks.

'The human embryo has a special status and we owe a measure of respect to the embryo. We also owe a measure of respect to the millions of people living with these devastating illnesses.'
Lord Hunt, Junior Health Minister, discussing the new law concerning research into human embryos in the UK, 2000

In complete contrast to the decision taken in the UK, the House of Representatives in the USA has voted to ban all human cloning. As a result, researchers will not be allowed to carry out research on embryos for any purpose, including therapeutic reasons. Anybody found to be flouting the new bill would be faced with heavy fines and a possible jail sentence.

'I don't think there's any way that you can prevent the creation of human clones without stopping it from the very beginning. We're talking about crossing a threshold here. We're no longer talking about using the quote-unquote excess embryo in the freezers for **stem cell** research. We're now talking about creating embryos for destructive research purposes.'
Representative Dave Weldon from Florida who sponsored the new bill in the House of Representatives

A right to an identity

One of the key issues with human cloning is the rights of cloned individuals to lead their own lives and have their own genetic identity. Dr Richard Seed, the US scientist who wants to set up the first human

Six rules

In 1995, John Habgood, former Archbishop of York, cautioned against using **genetic engineering** to improve people. He gave six rules that he believed society should follow: 'First, human beings are more than their **genes**. Genes are only a set of instructions. We are more than a set of instructions. Second rule: remember the valuable diversity of human nature. Third rule: look for justice in the dealings of human beings with one another and for fairness in the use of resources. Fourth rule: respect privacy and autonomy. Fifth rule: accept the presumption that diseases should be cured when it is possible to do so. And sixth rule: be very suspicious about improving human nature; and be even more suspicious of those who think they know what improvements ought to be made.'

clone clinic in Chicago, said he wished he had met Mother Teresa. He would have liked to have obtained a sample of her blood before she died from which to clone a replica saint. This is the very reason why many people are concerned about cloning. It raises many questions: What sort of life would such a baby have? Would people expect the child to grow up into the next Mother Teresa rather than be an individual in her own right? Would the child be owned by the clinic? The same problem would exist for a child who was a clone of their parent. The child would look like their father or their mother. But there is no guarantee that a clone would have the same personality as the original individual. Although clones are genetically identical, studies have shown that a person's personality and intelligence are affected by their environment. A clone many years younger than the original would be living in a different time, in different surroundings, eating different food and having a different education. All these factors would affect their personality so the clones may look identical but could behave very differently. Laws would need to be written to protect the rights of these individuals and to prevent their exploitation, but would have to be flexible enough to accommodate future scientific developments.

'I think cloning is a good idea in certain situations – when a man has no sperm cells it could help him have a child. I am collaborating with colleagues outside Italy who are carrying out animal experiments. This sort of research is banned here, but there is no doubt that cloning will be a reality within a few years.'

Professor Antinori, the controversial Italian infertility specialist, who has stated that he is ready to start cloning babies for infertile couples

Future developments

In the film *Jurassic Park*, a group of scientists recreated dinosaurs. They had supposedly found dinosaur **DNA** in the bodies of blood-sucking insects that had been preserved in amber. They had taken this DNA, repaired it, replaced the missing parts with DNA from reptiles and inserted it into an empty frog's egg. In the real world, there have been proposals to resurrect recently extinct animals, such as the dodo (a large, flightless bird) and the quagga (related to the zebra) using DNA from preserved specimens. The same idea has even been suggested in order to recreate dead celebrities such as Elvis Presley. Despite the advances in **gene** technology and cloning, this sort of possibility is still some way off – if indeed it is ever taken up.

An insect preserved in amber that is millions of years old. There is the theoretical possibility that the gut of a biting insect such as a mosquito, preserved in amber, could contain a minute amount of blood taken from an animal such as a dinosaur.

Growing hearts, livers and kidneys

A few years ago, Dr Charles Vacanti of the University of Massachusetts implanted a mould in the shape of a human ear on the back of a mouse. The mould was made of strands of a biodegradable plastic. Living human cartilage cells had been scattered over the mould where they grew and took on the shape of an ear. Eventually, the plastic mould broke down, leaving just the living cells. The mouse had been **genetically engineered** not to reject the human cells. Finally the ear was removed without killing the mouse. Thirty years from now, scientists will probably be growing whole hearts, livers and even limbs in high-tech labs. The organs will probably be grown in parts. For example, a heart would be built as valves, muscle and blood vessels, which would be joined together to form a heart. This means that one patient could have just part of their heart replaced – for example, faulty valves – while another could have their whole heart replaced.

Research teams have already successfully grown artificial bladders for dogs, using tissue taken from normal dogs' bladders. The cells were cultured in the lab so that there were plenty to use to make the new organ. Then the team made the support for the new organ in the form of 3D scaffolding in the shape of the bladder. This was seeded with bladder cells covered in specially formulated solutions. The cells started to grow and spread along the scaffolding until they reached the end, at which point they stopped growing. Once the tissue was in place, the scaffolding was designed to break down and disappear. The bladder took six weeks to grow and then it was **transplanted** into a dog. It functioned in the dog for eleven months. Similar techniques could be used to build hearts, livers and kidneys. However, these organs are more complex than a bladder and they will probably take several months to grow. The problems encountered by the team were making sure there was an adequate supply of oxygen and nutrients, and that the scaffolding enabled the cells to grow into the right shape.

It may prove possible to grow a whole limb ready for fitting on to a patient who has suffered an amputation. A whole limb offers a considerable challenge, however, since it is made up of many cell types which form different tissues. The scaffolding would have to be seeded with different cells and these cells would have to be persuaded to grow together.

Saving rare animals

More animals than ever before are now classed as being **endangered**. The causes are many – for example, the introduction of competitors, loss of natural habitat or poaching. There are some species so few in number that they are on the brink of extinction – for example, Spix's macaws and a sole surviving individual of a giant tortoise sub-species found on the Galapagos Islands. Some of these animals are old and unable to breed, so new individuals are unlikely to be born.

The Galapagos giant tortoise is an endangered species of reptile. The population of this species of tortoise is dangerously low and many of the animals are old.

It's not just wild animals that are under threat. Many indigenous breeds of livestock (those that orginate naturally in a region) are under threat from imported breeds that are being reared in intensive farming systems. The local breeds may contain valuable genes that confer heat tolerance or disease resistance and there is an urgent need to prevent their extinction. Currently, the method of conservation involves the storage of frozen **semen** or **embryos**, but this is time consuming and costly. As a result, only a small percentage of the species under threat are being protected in this way. Cloning may be the answer.

Animal cloning experiments

Experiments have already taken place with an endangered wild ox called a gaur found in India. The team took 692 skin cells from a dead gaur and fused them with cow's eggs that had had their nuclei removed. Of these, 40 developed into embryos and were placed in **surrogate** cows. Eight of these cows became pregnant and one calf was born. He was called Noah. Unfortunately, Noah died shortly after birth from a common bacterial infection that affects many newborn animals. An experiment planned for the future involves the bucardo or Spanish mountain goat. Unfortunately, the last surviving bucardo was killed by a falling tree. Tissue samples were taken and she will be cloned. However, all the clones will be female. **Chromosomes** from the goat species that is most closely related to the bucardo will be needed to create a male mountain goat.

Frozen for the future

Each cell of an animal's body contains the full **genetic code** for the whole animal and **nuclear transfer** provides a way of converting cells to whole animals. Cells from endangered breeds, collected from scrapings of the soft skin inside the mouth or from **hair follicles**, would be multiplied in the laboratory and frozen. The frozen cells could be stored indefinitely at $-173\,°C$ in liquid nitrogen. This is called cryo-preservation. At some time in the future, a living population of animals could be re-established from the frozen cells using the same procedures that created Dolly.

Cryo-preservation is a method of storing cell and tissue samples for long periods of time. The samples are frozen and stored in special cannisters at -173°C in liquid nitrogen.

Endangered populations with only a few breeding individuals are at risk from inbreeding, that is, related animals breeding with each other. This reduces genetic diversity. If a few of the individuals carry harmful genes, then there is a greater likelihood of these genes spreading through the population. In a larger population, the genes would be 'diluted' and have less of an effect on the health of the animals. Inbreeding tends to produce less healthy animals that have a reduced resistance to disease. The same is true of cloning: all the individuals are the same, so there is no genetic diversity. The problem could be partly solved by taking samples from as many different individuals as possible.

'If you produce lots of animals that are identical, you get inbreeding. They can't adapt to stresses, which is what evolution is about and why you need biological diversity.'

Bill Holt of the Zoological Society of London, talking about the problems of a lack of diversity among clones of a single animal

The advantages of cloning

Cloning has many advantages over the current methods of obtaining **sperm** and embryos. The collection of sperm and eggs from wild animals requires special skills and equipment. There is also an element of risk to the animal itself as it usually has to be sedated or even anaesthetized. The number of embryos that are produced in this way is small and there is the risk that none of the embryos will survive when they are eventually used. In contrast, the collection of cells for cryo-preservation would be relatively simple and could be done in the field without any special expertise. Also, cloning provides an unlimited supply of cells with which to keep trying for a successful pregnancy.

Cloning alone will not save rare species, but it is one way of saving these species until a better way forward is found and the reasons for the animals' decline are addressed. However, there would be little point in cloning a whole new group of endangered animals if, because of human destruction, they had no habitat in which to live. For example, the giant panda feeds on bamboo so it is found only in forests where there is bamboo. These forests are disappearing rapidly and this is threatening its survival. The cells of the giant panda could be frozen but there would be no point in recreating giant pandas if there was nowhere for them to live. Similarly, some of the rarest macaws live in tropical rainforests. Not only is the rainforest being cleared, but the macaws are trapped and sold as pets. It would be pointless producing expensive clones of macaws for release back into the wild if they were to be caught by poachers. It could be necessary to keep the tissues of some endangered species in storage for several hundred years.

'As a last ditch effort for conservation, it might be useful. But it would be daft to imagine that cloning alone could save species.'

Gordon Reid, Director of Chester Zoo, talking about cloning

Advanced Cell Technology

One of the leading teams in cloning is based at a company called Advanced Cell Technology in the USA. This team is led by Philip Damiani. This team has had many successes including cloning an adult leg cell (see page 37), producing the gaur Noah and trying to save the burcardo (see page 51). They have also created embryos of endangered African wild cats and of Indian desert cats, using eggs taken from domestic cats. They have successfully implanted the embryos in the wombs of domestic cat surrogate mothers, but have yet to achieve a long-term pregnancy. However, Philip Damiani does not believe that cloning will solve all the problems of rare animals. His team has been carrying out cloning experiments to prove that it can be done and applied to endangered species. He envisages 'frozen zoos' where tissues from endangered species such as the gaur and giant panda could be stored. If their numbers fell to dangerously low levels then the tissues could be used to produce clones and increase genetic diversity.

The gaur is an endangered species of wild ox that is found in India. Taking tissue samples from some of the remaining animals and storing them for future use could be one way of ensuring the survival of this ox.

Designer babies

Within the next 20 to 30 years, the technology will probably exist to enable people to 'design their own baby'. By then scientists may know the position and sequence of every human gene and how they interact with each other. Already, doctors can take a cell from an unborn child and test the DNA for some genetic diseases. Techniques have been developed to genetically alter sperm cells in animals to ensure that specific characteristics are inherited in the offspring. Soon, it will be possible to do this to human sperm. Initially, embryos produced by *in vitro* **fertilization** would be altered to eliminate unwanted genes, but there is the potential to do much more. People might feel that it would be acceptable to remove genes responsible for genetic diseases such as cystic fibrosis, muscular dystrophy or haemophilia. But would it be acceptable to enhance traits such as creativity, athletic or musical ability?

Enhancement isn't necessarily a good thing. There is a genetically engineered strain of fruit fly that learns ten times faster than normal flies. Imagine humans with enhanced memories and learning ability. It would mean that people could take their exams after a few months study and wouldn't forget as much. But psychologists consider that it is important to be able to forget the unpleasant experiences of life. There is even some evidence to suggest that people who have total recall of events or information or a photographic memory are at a disadvantage. They can remember events that happened some time ago as vividly as if they happened yesterday and this can be very confusing for them.

There is, of course, a significant risk of people abusing the technology of cloning. In a world where money is important, it is possible that rich parents would demand that genetic engineering was carried out on their unborn child to make them perfect, at least in their eyes. But who is to be the judge of what or who is perfect? And what would happen if something went wrong? Would the parents blame the doctor who carried out the alterations?

The whole subject of human cloning and 'designer babies' raises many **ethical** and moral questions. Many of the predictions may seem far-fetched and applicable only to a science fiction movie, but there are lots of realities today that were equally unthinkable to people of previous generations.

Conclusion

When science presents something new, the most common reaction is fear. The first baby produced by IVF, Louise Brown, was born in 1978. At that time the technique was extremely controversial. Two decades on and IVF is now commonplace. Thirty years ago people were worried about **recombinant DNA** – the beginnings of **genetic engineering**. There were even more worries when the first genetically modified (engineered) crops were grown. But genetic engineering is slowly becoming part of our daily lives. And people's initial reaction to cloning is the same – fear.

The arrival of Dolly focused the world's attention on the issues of cloning. Some people argue that these discussions should have been made before breakthroughs such as the creation of Dolly actually occurred. But it's impossible to predict all the potential developments of a technology. Developments such as the cloning of high-quality livestock will probably proceed without much response from the public. Very few people seem to object to the use of cloning in the conservation of **endangered** animals, although they may have a very different opinion if asked about the re-creation of extinct animals.

However, it's the topics of human **stem cell** research and human **reproductive cloning** that are generating the most fear. Most governments have already put into place a temporary ban on these fields of research. This is creating a 'breathing space' so that these controversial subjects can be properly debated. However, there are many people who say it would be a mistake to rush to ban *any* research into human cloning. If research is completely banned, many of the benefits would be lost. History shows that however beneficial some technological developments can be to society as a whole, there will always be ways in which they can be misused. Already people talk of the threat of dictators cloning themselves. But, dictators do not need clones to carry out their cruel policies, they use the power of their armies and bully tactics to get their way. The solution is not to regulate the technology itself, but to regulate its application.

This is why it is so important that governments have balanced legislation in place. In many countries, licences are needed to carry out research on human **embryos** and the licence-holders are not allowed to place a cloned embryo into a **uterus**. The UK government, along with many others, has indicated that it will outlaw any human reproductive cloning. Whatever happens, it is important that all the issues are carefully considered before making decisions that could affect the future of us all.

Looking ahead, it is likely that at some point in the near future humans will be cloned, but it will probably not be called cloning. Cloning is a word that provokes emotional reactions, so it is likely that scientists will probably use another phrase such as **nuclear transfer**. Meanwhile, society as a whole has time to contemplate which uses of the technology might be acceptable and which would not.

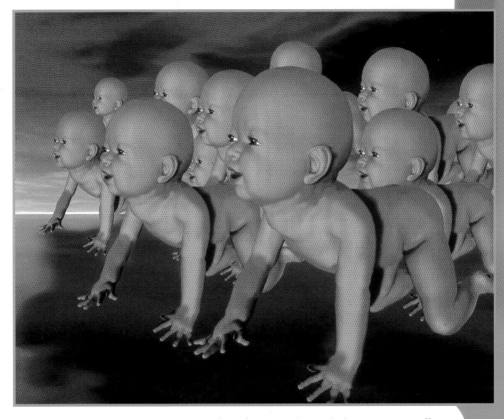

This is one artist's vision of the future – identical clones coming off the production line. Will there ever be human clones? Scientists and non-scientists will have to decide what is acceptable and what is not.

Timeline

1860s Discovery of **chromosomes** in a cell's nucleus.

1880s August Weismann, Professor of Zoology at the University of Freiburg, Germany, suggests that the passing of hereditary material takes place when chromosomes divide during cell division.

1938 Hans Spemann, German **embryologist**, publishes his book, entitled *Embryonic Development and Induction*.

1952 American embryologists Robert Briggs and Tom King successfully remove a **nucleus** from a frog **embryo** and place it in an egg which has had its nucleus removed. The embryo continues to develop.

1963 British biologist J.B.S. Haldane becomes the first person to use the term 'clone' (a Greek word meaning 'twig') in a speech entitled 'Biological possibilities for the human species in the next 10,000 years'. Until this time, researchers had referred to cloning as nuclear transplantation.

1969 American biologists James Shapiro and Jonathan Beckwith announce that they have isolated the first **gene**, a bacterial gene that is used to digest milk sugar.

1971 James Watson, co-discoverer of the structure of **DNA**, testifies to the US Congress that scientists will soon be able to clone human beings.

British biologists Patrick Steptoe and Robert Edwards start developing a technique called *in vitro* **fertilization**.

1978 Louise Brown, the world's first test-tube baby, is born in the UK.

1986 Danish scientist Steen Willadsen, working in Cambridge, announces that he has cloned sheep from early embryo cells.

1987 American scientists Randall Prather and Neal First announce the arrival of cloned cows, also produced by transferring a nucleus from an embryo into an egg cell.

1990 Human Genome Project involving teams of scientists around the world is set up.

1995 Morag and Megan, two cloned sheep that had been **genetically engineered** to produce human drugs, are born at the Roslin Institute.

1996 Dolly the sheep, the first clone of an adult cell, is born at the Roslin Institute.

1997 Polly the sheep, a sheep that carries a human gene, is born at the Roslin Institute.

1998 Advanced Cell Technology, a US company, announces that it has successfully cloned human cells.

Birth of the first cloned transgenic cow, a calf named Victoria. Transgenic animals have been given genes taken from other organisms.

2000 Advanced Cell Technology announces that it has an agreement with the Spanish government to clone the extinct bucardo, a type of mountain goat.

2001 Advanced Cell Technology announces the birth of a baby gaur (**endangered** wild ox) called Noah, but he dies a few days later.

The House of Commons in the UK votes to allow controversial research on embryos. The creation of clones of human cells for research into serious diseases is permitted.

Research teams publish the first working draft of the **genetic code** of the human genome.

Italian **infertility** specialist, Professor Antinori, announces that he will be ready to clone babies within the next two years.

Cyagra, the livestock division of Advanced Cell Technology, announces the birth of cloned calves. These are clones of a cow named Zita who was the top ranked Holstein cow in the USA in 1997. She produced nearly double the national average amounts of milk and butterfat.

2002 Scientists debate the news that Dolly the sheep has arthritis. It is not known if this is part of the natural ageing process, or caused by the process of cloning.

Glossary

antibody special protein made by the immune system that attaches to any foreign cells and inactivates them

artificial insemination transfer of sperm from a male to a female in order to fertilize an egg without sexual intercourse

bone marrow liquid-like tissue, found in the centre of the body's largest bones, that produces red blood cells, white blood cells and platelets

chromosome one of the thread-like structures in a nucleus, made up of DNA and protein. Chromosomes become visible during cell division. Each chromosome may carry many different genes. There are 23 pairs of chromosomes in a human cell, except in red blood cells, which have no chromosomes, and the sex cells. Sex cells (sperm and egg) are produced in a special kind of cell division in which the chromosome number halves. They have 23 single chromosomes. Without this reduction in the number of chromosomes, they would double with every generation.

cellulose a carbohydrate that forms a wall around plant cells

cytoplasm jelly-like substance which fills the cell and in which the components of the cell are suspended

DNA (deoxyribonucleic acid) molecule that carries the genetic code, found in the nucleus

donor someone who donates an organ or a product of their body – for example, bone marrow – to help someone who has a faulty organ or product

embryo term for an egg after it has been fertilized, when it is in its early stages of development

embryology the study of embryos

encryption the conversion of data into a code so that it cannot be read or accessed by an unauthorized person

endangered term for a species that is at risk of becoming extinct (that is, dying out)

enzyme type of protein produced by living cells that is able to catalyse (increase the speed of) reactions within organisms

ethical to do with what is morally right or wrong

fertilization joining together of a male and female sex cell to form a new individual

gene unit of inheritance that is passed on from parent to offspring, made up of a length of DNA on a chromosome

genetic code sequence of chemical bases in DNA and RNA which codes for specific amino acids

genetic engineering (also called genetic modification) production of new combinations of genetic material by altering the DNA of an organism. Usually a gene from one organism is introduced into the DNA of another.

genetics the study of heredity, how different characteristics are inherited

growth medium solution (containing nutrients) on which organisms such as bacteria are grown

hair follicle small group of cells that surround and feed a hair

HIV (human immunodeficiency virus) virus responsible for AIDS (acquired immune deficiency syndrome). It is transmitted through the exchange of body fluids, primarily semen, blood and blood products.

immune system system in the body that recognizes foreign cells and destroys them

infertile unable to produce offspring

in vitro **fertilization** (IVF) medical process in which an egg from a woman is fertilized in a glass Petri dish (in vitro means 'in glass') in the laboratory. The resulting embryo is then implanted in her uterus.

leukaemia cancer that affects the white blood cells

molecule smallest unit a chemical substance can be divided into while still having the properties of that substance

nuclear transfer transferring of a nucleus from one cell and placing it an empty egg cell. The egg cell is then stimulated into dividing to produce an embryo.

nucleus central part of a cell, which controls many cell functions and contains the DNA

Parkinson's progressive disease of the nervous system, in which sufferers have difficulty controlling their muscle movements

photosynthesis process by which plants manufacture sugars and starch using carbon dioxide and water, in the presence of light. The process takes place in the chloroplasts which contain a green pigment called chlorophyll.

protein a large molecule made from amino acids. It is important for growth and repair. Protein-rich foods include meat, dairy produce, eggs and fish.

recombinant DNA DNA that has been stitched together using DNA from different sources, for example removing DNA for a human gene and inserting it into the DNA of a bacterium

reproductive cloning cloning cells to produce embryos which will be allowed to develop into a new individual

semen mixture of sperm and fluids produced by male mammals when they ejaculate (discharge semen)

sexual reproduction fusion of gametes (egg and sperm) to create offspring that are different from their parents and from each other

sperm male sex cell

stem cell 'immortal' cell that retains the ability to divide and multiply and to create other types of cell. Stem cells are found in embryos, bone marrow, skin, intestine and muscle tissue.

surrogate female animal that gives birth to another female's baby

therapeutic cloning cloning cells for the treatment of medical conditions and diseases

transplant to take a tissue or an organ from a donor and use it to replace a diseased tissue or organ in another individual

uterus (also called the womb) organ of the female reproductive system in which the foetus (unborn child) grows and develops

Sources of information

Further reading

Many magazines such as *New Scientist* and *Biological Review* and newspapers such as the *Guardian* write about cloning in an accessible manner.

Websites

www.advancedcell.com (Advanced Cell Technology)
Website of the company that has produced a wide range of cloned animals including Noah, the first endangered animal clone.

www.humancloning.org (The Human Cloning Foundation)
This is a foundation in favour of human cloning. It has a lot of information about human cloning, including a Help for Students section.

www.newscientist.com (New Scientist magazine)
Many articles on cloning can be found here.

www.roslin.co.uk (Roslin Institute)
This website is run by the institute where Dolly was created. You can find a lot of background information on cloning and genetic engineering here plus useful links to other sites.

www.royalsoc.ac.uk (Royal Society)
Here you can find policy documents on a range of subjects including therapeutic cloning using stem cells.

www.sciam.com (Scientific American magazine)
This website contains many features on cloning.

Author sources

The author used the following materials in the writing of this book:

Applied Genetics, Geoff Hayward (Nelson, 1992)

Clone: The Road to Dolly and the Path Ahead, Gina Kolata (Penguin Books, 1997)

Improving Nature? The Science and Ethics of Genetic Engineering, Michael J. Reiss and Roger Straughton (Cambridge University Press, 1996)

Stem Cell Research and Therapeutic Cloning: an update, Royal Society Policy Document (November, 2000)

The Engineer in the Garden, Colin Tudge (Pimlico, 1995)

Magazines – *Biological Review, Focus, Nature, New Scientist, Science, Scientific American*

Index

Titles in the *Science at the Edge* series:

Hardback   0 431 14885 6

Hardback   0 431 14882 1

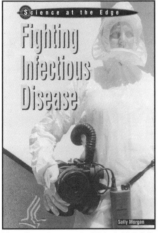

Hardback   0 431 14884 8

Hardback   0 431 14883 X

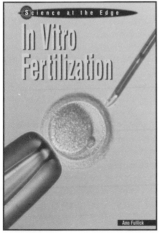

Hardback   0 431 14881 3

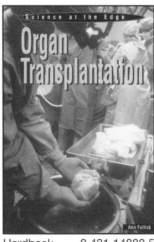

Hardback   0 431 14880 5

Find out about other Heinemann Library titles on our website www.heinemann.co.uk/library